#MINDSET

A MINDSET OF *change.*

DERRON ROWAN

WEALTH PROSPER QUEEN FUTURE VALUED SUCCESS FIT BELIEVE WINNER MENTOR FORGIVING GRATEFUL SURVIVOR HUSTLE

#MINDSET
A MINDSET OF *change.*

INSPIRED MOTIVATED GOD TRUST POSITIVE LOVE KING STRONG MOGUL VIRTUOUS QUEEN GROWTH CREATIVE

XULON PRESS

Xulon Press
2301 Lucien Way #415
Maitland, FL 32751
407.339.4217
www.xulonpress.com

© 2020 by Derron Rowan

All rights reserved solely by the author. The author guarantees all contents are original and do not infringe upon the legal rights of any other person or work. No part of this book may be reproduced in any form without the permission of the author. The views expressed in this book are not necessarily those of the publisher.

Book Cover design by Screenshot Studios Michelle Ignacia
Email: officialscreenshots@gmail.com

Photograph done by Rodney Pitts Photography:
Email muddog20@gmail.com

Unless otherwise indicated, Scripture quotations taken from the Holy Bible, New International Version (NIV). Copyright © 1973, 1978, 1984, 2011 by Biblica, Inc.™. Used by permission. All rights reserved.

Printed in the United States of America

Paperback ISBN-13: 978-1-6322-1071-5
Ebook ISBN-13: 978-1-6322-1072-2

FORWARD FOR #MINDSET

At the height of the Great Recession, Hannah Rosin wrote a fascinating article for the Atlantic entitled "The End of Men" wherein she articulated a compelling argument as to the ways that the Great Recession has challenged and rearranged the way that men, in particular, approach life, love and work. A decade later, Derron Rowan, has unintentionally given the world a response through his provocative work, #Mindset! This book holds the power to change the trajectories of individuals whom have been disillusioned by the quick changes and startling challenges that life presents whether those challenges are presented by financial shifts brought about by the global economy, relationship dysfunction or career setbacks. Derron Rowan gets it right that overcoming obstacles and arriving at the next level is totally depended on one's mindset. To be successful at shifting mindset is to open the door to new possibilities. I highly commend this book to everyone who is interested in experiencing how a shift in mindset can radically change their life!

Dr. Corrie Shull
Louisville, Kentucky

#Mindset

From My Dad:

I was young and now I'm old, in my youth at the age of 20 years old, my wife Lena and I had this wonderful 8lbs 14 oz. baby boy. We named him Derron. He loved playing with footballs and running around the building in all kinds of weather. He finally hit the corner of the building and busted his head and had to go to the health care center and get stitches. It took 6 nurses to hold him down. Derron has always been an ambitious achiever from elementary school to high school, ROTC and college. Derron has a special gift for writing poetry, the performing arts and is a aspiring actor. Derron is an inspiration to all who truly know him and you too will be auspiciously blessed when you leap into the pages of this book . Love you son...Dad

Forward For #mindset

Who am I?

My name is Derron Rowan. You can also call me Dee Rowan. I am a native of Louisville, Kentucky, which is the birthplace of the G.O.A.T. Muhammad Ali. I have two beautiful daughters, Weslie and Jazlyn, who have been my "why" for many inspirational moments along this journey. I am proud to have finally written this book after many, many attempts to start it. Starting was the most challenging part for me because I lacked the belief that I could do it. I was missing the confidence to share with you my story and that of others which will hopefully and prayerfully inspire you to reach your goals and follow through on your vision. A dream is just a vision until you make it into reality. So, I hope you enjoy this manuscript in all its transparency. I pray that it inspires you to examine your mindset for change. I myself attempt to challenge my mindset every day to be better, to think higher, and to strive for more.

Thank you,
Derron Rowan

INTRODUCTION

As you read this book, you will come across a quick sentence that says, "Clap for yourself." When you see this, just stop reading and simply clap for yourself! Thank you for taking the time to read this script. You all have played a major role in my life, and I thank you. I hope you enjoy it.

When birthing my apparel brand #Mindset, I had no idea of the impact the brand would have. How would I market it? How would I give power to people to be proud of the season they are in, coming out of, or heading into? Each season we encounter is a testimony and has the power to strengthen someone else if we can be open about it and share. I chose two tag lines when branding #Mindset Apparel. One was, "Encouraging your mindset every day," and the other was, "Daily Growth and Abundance," (my daughter Jaz actually helped me with the tags—thank you).

We go through so much and experience many ups and downs in our lives. It can be overwhelming, and it definitely takes a toll on our mental health. I hope that #Mindset is a brand that people can relate to and feel a sense of pride about with what they are wearing on their bodies—to display the season they are heading into in their lives and show confirmation of the season they just left that didn't kill them but maybe encouraged them.

#Mindset

How can we change our mindset? Here are some pointers below that I pray will help you as they did me, which I continue to work on daily:

1. Meditate. I am still a work in progress here, as in many areas, but meditating is one of the greatest tools we can do to clear our mind and focus on what we need to for the moment, the day, the week, or whatever.

2. Listen to podcasts. When I realized the valuable time I had wasted over my career commuting back and forth for two hours round trip and mainly just listening to the same old music over and over again, it upset me, so I started to listen to different podcasts. I have my favorites, which range from motivational to spiritual topics and others about prosperity, life lessons, and encouragement. The point is that I wanted to give my mind some new food to digest so I could begin to grow different fruit. I still like to listen to my music; I just have a better balance now. Your mind is a muscle. You have to feed it the right foods to digest and allow it to flourish.

3. Brag on yourself. Every day when I come home from work, I write something positive about myself down. Then I post it where I can see it. I got this idea from the TV show "Being Mary Jane." In it, the main character places inspirational Post-it notes all over her house to serve as reminders to herself. I have Post-it notes everywhere at home now and even at work. My good friend jokes with me about ordering so many Post-it notes at a time, but it's important to me to always see positivity and to be reminded that I can and I will. We focus on the negative so much during our busy lives. How many times do you actually praise yourself for the great job you did today? Maybe it was just something small and didn't matter to anyone else, but when you

Introduction

write that thing down, it will mean something to you. And that's what is important.

4. Focus on your short-term and long-term goals. You determine what to celebrate and the timeline. Sometimes we need to appreciate the small things to appreciate the larger things in life. Some of us are not in the #mindset to plan out a long-term goal, and that is okay. Plan your goal according to your level.

5. Make your development a priority. Dedicate time to being better, affording yourself that time to read, research things that interest you, or sit alone if you just need to be quiet. I have a friend who watches movies on mute but turns on the closed captions. I remember asking her, "Why do you do that?" She replied, "It's relaxing." At the time, I was like, "Uh huh, okay…" But now when I look at it, it's a form of meditation. Yes, the movie is playing and the words are on the screen, but it's quiet and allows your brain to slow down and relax.

6. Elevate your surroundings. This also means your friends. Some people cannot go where you are going because they only know you for where you are now. If you have friends who constantly see you as who you were and can never find it in themselves to acknowledge and celebrate the you who you are trying to become, then maybe, just maybe, those friendships have run their course.

I want 2020 to be about growth and abundance. I lost too much in 2018 and 2019. I have declared this year my year of new beginnings. It is not going to be easy, but hell, 2018 and 2019 weren't easy either!

#Mindset

Want to know a secret? The devil knows how to get your attention. He knows your patterns and knows what moves you in this direction or that. The devil will learn our patterns and mistakes faster than we can, and that's how he knows how to attack us.

What about in your life? What do you want out of 2020? What did you lose in the last years that made you say on December 31, 2019, "Enough is enough!"? We have to start somewhere, people, and until we change our minds, nothing else will matter. We will just be walking in frustration if we don't adjust our mentality first. We have to believe that we can be more, that we can obtain more. You have to believe that you are more, that you don't have to settle, that you don't have to be in that negative situation anymore, and that you are worthy.

Clap for yourself!

#MINDSET

CHAPTER 1
#BELIEFMINDSET

So, this is actually chapter 23. Yeah, I know the page says chapter 1, but trust me, it's not lol. I have started this book over more times than I can count—thinking about what to say, when to say it, and how to say it. Than someone said to me, "Just write it and don't care about your spelling or your grammar. All that can be fixed. Just start writing." Thank you, Ton'e Brown.

I decided to name the book *#Mindset*. I choose that title because going through so much in 2018 and 2019, I knew something had to change. I knew that to have a better year—not even a great year but a better year—I had to change some things up. I knew I had to grow mentally, and to do that, I had to focus on my mindset. I wanted to be more faithful with my Bible studies and spending time with God. I mean, I was trying to do a complete overhaul of myself, my brand, my character, and my attitude. The more I tried to change some things, though, the more I found there was resistance—not so much from anyone else but from me. I became my biggest competition, my biggest doubter, and my biggest fear-of-change component. Many times, we are so worried about others on the outside being a danger to us, but the real fight is against the enemy in you—en-a-me. It is a shame that we can defeat ourselves out of our own growth.

#Mindset

Self-doubt is one of the biggest reasons people cannot and will not change in life. I read a blog by Henrik Edberg which discussed this, titled, "13 Powerful Ways to Overcome Self-doubt (So You Can Finally Move Forward in Life)." William Shakespeare said, "Our doubts are traitors, and make us lose the good we oft might win, by fearing to attempt." Wow, do you need to read that again? Go ahead—I'll wait! I mean Shakespeare said our doubts are traitors. What is a traitor? A traitor is "a person who betrays a friend, a principle, a country, etc."—a double-crosser. Have you ever thought of yourself as a traitor? Sometimes we are quick to call someone a traitor when we think he or she has wronged us or done something to harm us. But have you ever thought of yourself as a traitor—the inner you working against yourself to keep you from the good you "oft might win by fearing to attempt"? That was exactly what I was fighting against for my personal growth.

I took some time off to work on some issues within me. I sought counsel, which was a different experience that I'll discuss later. But after my divorce from my wife and all the other things going on, I had to separate to learn to relate with myself. I did not like me, and I didn't like the direction I was going in. But before I get too far off track, let's talk about this blog I read from Mr. Henrik Edberg. In it, he listed thirteen powerful ways to overcome self-doubt:

1. Say stop.

When that self-doubt even begins to start, quickly recognize it and say, "Stop! No, no, no—we are not going down that road again." "By doing this you can disrupt your thought pattern and stop that inner self-doubt from taking over."

2. Look to the past and awash yourself in the memories.

#beliefmindset

"Be real with yourself (I like this part) and ask yourself: How many times when I doubted myself or feared something would happen did that negative thing come into reality after I still took action?" Probably not many times at all, right? Yeah, this is me asking you this question—sorry! But really, how many times when you doubted yourself did the negative thing you were doubting happen to you? Henrick says that if you look to the past and see how well things have gone many times despite those self-doubts, then it becomes easier to let go or ignore them and focus on the more likely positive outcome and take action. It then becomes you shifting your energy to believe in yourself rather than the outside factors surrounding you.

3. Talk to someone about it.

"When you keep your thoughts on the inside, they can become distorted, exaggerated and not very much in line with reality or reasonable expectations."

Ha, this is where I will tell my story that I told you I would get back to. I am going to be very transparent in some of my comments here, so do not judge me. Well, I am putting it in a book, so I obviously do not care what you judge! So, the separation from my wife was very damn difficult, despite what some may say. There were days when I felt paralyzed. I didn't want to get out of bed; I didn't want to hang with my friends. I barely wanted to see my parents, and I all but avoided my daughters. The only thing I wanted to do (and I didn't even really want to do this) was go to work and come home and pass out. That process was overwhelming, and my emotions some days were too much to bear. Loss of appetite, loss of energy, and wanting to be alone became my new normal. Crying some nights until my pillow was soaked was like sitting in a hot sauna. Walking into work every day, knowing I had to put on a brave face, was a challenge. My temperament was short, my emotions stayed on high, and some of my decisions were questionable. One night at work, I had a total breakdown in the breakroom. I ended up leaving work after I opened up to my manager about what was going on. I had an hour-long drive home from work, and the whole way, I ain't going to lie, I had several bad thoughts. But I am so thankful the Lord kept me that night. I knew I had to see someone and couldn't continue on the same path.

I decided to seek counsel. I knew there were some attitudes and dysfunctions in my personality that I needed to conquer and change. I remember when I called the helpline at work, which was a service we could use that would allow our insurance to pay for a certain amount of sessions with a counselor. I hung up on the lady who answered the phone at least three times before I could even ask for the next step or a counselor's name. Hell, on the third time, she called me back. I forgot everyone has caller ID now! So, I made the appointment and went to my first visit. I walked into the office and checked in. There were two other people there. The clerk asked, "May I help you?" and I leaned all the way to the other side of the desk where she was sitting and said, "I have a 12:30 appointment," in a quiet, mouse-like voice.

She cracked a smile and said, "Okay, I got you." I just wanted to keep things quiet, you know, because the office was quiet. I felt like she knew I was a little embarrassed by the way I checked in because she'd whispered back, "I got you." I thought, *Cool*. I had my hat pulled down on my head, I'd parked deep in the parking lot, and I was dressed casual so as not to draw attention to myself, so I was being discreet. I sat there in that cozy waiting area, talking myself out of keeping my appointment. I probably went through more mind changes than Peyton Manning did when he would call audibles (football fans will get the reference!), but I stayed. Plus, the clerk had said she'd got me.

#beliefmindset

Well, at 12:30, it was my time for the appointment. The clerk slid that window open and said, "Derron Rowan, your counselor will see you now."

I thought, *What the hell is wrong with you, lady? I thought you said you had me!* I looked up, and the other people in the office did not pay me any mind. They were dealing with their own issues that had brought them there. So, I headed back to the office to meet my counselor. When I walked in, he was a man, dressed in the latest fashion with designer shoes. He did not have a ring on his finger (yes, I noticed all that), and he sat with his legs crossed, looking at me. So, as he was going through all the preliminary stuff like name, work, address, etc., I was scoping out the office. I did not see any family pics, neither male nor female, and no damn ring—just a bunch of books and a Facebook icon on his computer. At this point, I just decided I had wasted an hour and was not going to tell him anything. So, we literally sat there for a good forty-five minutes. Yes, he asked questions, but after a while, he was like, "Derron, if you do not talk, I can't help."

"I was like, dude, I am not telling you jack." To be judged by a man, to be exposed, to be thought of as weak—nah, my brother, just bill my insurance and collect this easy check! I was not about to let him put me on some meds and label me.

This childish behavior of mine lasted one more session. Then I finally started to talk to him after some reassurances. And you know what? It was actually helpful. I was really able to deal with some issues that were lying dormant in my life but were holding me captive at the same time. We talked, I cried; we talked, I sobbed; we talked, I laughed; we talked, I healed. Henrik Edberg says, "Just letting them out and saying them out loud can offer to help you to hear how exaggerated these thoughts have become, and by talking about those doubts with someone that is supportive you can get a change of perspective." I can honestly say I benefitted from seeing the counselor. I just let it all out. I was like, "Judge me if you want, but I need to make a change in my life, and you about to earn every penny!" Now, for my men who think going to see a counselor is a sign of weakness, I say now that *not* going to see a counselor is a sign of weakness. Some of us use the barber chair and the folks in it as counseling sessions. Although it's fun, fellows having barbershop talk while draped in the cape does not cut it. Seeking help did not make me any less of a man, nor did it take my man card. Just the opposite—I was able to find some things in me that pushed me back on track to becoming the man that I needed to be, the man I was intended to be, the man I wanted to be. I was able to find out some things within me that had been dormant, and then I found out some things about me that I had to kill. I had some demons that I needed to be delivered from. So, men, go and talk to someone if you must. You are still a man, but are you the man you want to be—the man that you deserve, that others deserve?

Clap for yourself!

4. Do not get stuck in the comparison trap.

"If you compare yourself to other people all too often to their successes and especially to their high light reels that they share on social media then self-doubt can quickly creep up." Omg, isn't that the truth? How many times do you see people post something and be like, "Dang, they got it going on!" They seem to have everything so together, like they don't have a care in the world. I mean, honestly, you cannot help but admire some people. Even if you don't have a jealous bone in your body, always seeing someone win can be exhausting. Henrik warns against this and simply says to, "Compare yourself against yourself to see how far you have come." Do this to see how you have grown as an adult and as a human being. Did you have parents who would mark your growth against the wall as a child? Weekly, they would say, "Come here. Let's see how much you have grown." Whether you grew an inch or stayed the same, it was okay. It was just to see how much you'd grown. The same can be done in our adult lives. We can use factors, indicators, and milestones to mark our growth. We can take note on where we are and how we feel and then use these as reflections—not to challenge ourselves but to see our areas of growth and stagnation.

5. Keep a journal.

I did this for myself at the advice of my counselor. Keeping a journal allowed me to keep my focus and reflect on how the day went overall. I used it to manage my growth and my weaknesses in areas. But this only works if you are honest with yourself.

6. Remember that people don't care that much about what you do or say.

"When you worry about what others may think or say if you do something then the self-doubt-can quickly become stronger and you get stuck in inaction and in fear." I refer to my story of when I went to the counselor's office. I was so embarrassed to even make the phone call at first. Thank God the clerk called me back after I'd hung up on her three times! I would have also missed my blessing if the people in the counselor office had cared as much about me as I thought they did because I would have walked out of that office and never gone to a session, only delaying my path to healing and re-branding.

7. What someone said or did might not be about you (or about what you think it is).

"You don't know everything that is going on in another person's life. And the world doesn't revolve around you." Just like yo mama used to say: "Boy/girl, the world will go on without you. It still spins." So be careful you don't misinterpret and build blame and doubt within, without a reason.

8. Get a boost of optimism.

"Let someone else's enthusiasm, motivation and constructive optimism flow over to you." I had to switch up what I was watching, listening to, and interacting with. Negative energy is contagious, just like positive energy. I remember when we lived in a very nice, affluent neighborhood where everyone's grass was maintained meticulously. We had a new family move in between us and another neighbor. The new homeowners did not take as good of care of their yard as the other neighbor and me. I was cutting twice a week, trimming shrubs once a month, applying the right amount of grass fertilizer, edging—I did it all. Heck, I even had to start putting my mower in the shop during the off-season because my neighbors said I needed my blades sharpened to help the blades of grass look uniform! One Saturday morning, I overheard my two neighbors exchanging words. The neighbor who had been there longer was telling the newer neighbor that his lack of care of his own yard was making it hard on him and me to take care of our yards. The newer neighbor asked how this could be. So, the neighbor politely explained to him that bad grass spreads just like a cold or a virus if left untreated. He showed him how his grass at the grass line of the newer neighbor's yard did not look like a commercial anymore but instead looked a lot like his, full of—untreated, unhealthy, brown, spotty, and, honestly, ugly. The newer neighbor understood, and from then on, he put more effort into his yard than I did! The point had been made. Now, isn't that a lot like what we deal with on a human level? People's bad attitudes and experiences and negative energy can spew into our lives if we are not careful, and if we let things go untreated, they become unhealthy. There is a saying that you should be happy when the Lord is blessing someone you know, because that means he is on your street, and your blessing is on the way.

9. See a setback as temporary.

Henrik says, "This way of looking at things can trap you in thinking that there's no point in continuing to take action. Remember you are not a failure just because you failed, setbacks happen to everyone who takes chances, it is simply a part of living life fully." I have always been a risk taker, and I have failed many, many times in business ventures, and life. I would encourage you to take notes or use a journal to document your experiences that your go through. This will help you in each test you take and fail, and also your wins, just to be able to reflect. But I think it's important to say, for me at least, that you won't know if you don't try. There is a vision, greatness, and higher calling in each of us. But if you don't try, you will never know, and one day, you will say, "I wish I would have at least tried." Give me 100 failures at trying rather than one regret and saying, "I played it safe." Setbacks or just setups for God to show up and show out in our lives. How many times have you wanted to try something, but fear of failing paralyzed you. How my times in your life, when you knew you had that great idea, but you became afraid to pull the action to make it a reality for you, only to come across the same idea later in your life and someone else is making it successful. We have to stop letting the setbacks become permanent in us, and learn to reset, and recalibrate from that moment of failure and see it as a lesson. A lesson that we should use to catapult us toward confidence for our next event in our lives. Job loss, car loss, homes being lost, credit is weak, dropped out of school, relationships don't pan out, divorce, all these setbacks are temporary. That aren't fatal, they aren't a life sentence to stay in exile and wallow in depression, we can rebound from the setbacks we experience and move with assurance that we can succeed.

10. Sharpen your skills.

Use some of your free time to strengthen your weaknesses and be honest with yourself about your shortcomings. Listen to podcasts, attend seminars, and watch YouTube videos. Find a way to make your skillset stronger so you will be strong and confident when called upon to use it. My Grandfather use to say, "You can pull out of you, what you don't put in you" Simple right? A skill I undervalued was reading. But as I got older, I realized the wealth of knowledge that was within the covers of a book. Now we have the luxury of using modern technology to let books read to us. Pretty soon Alexa will be reading books to us at our request.

11. Don't beat yourself up.

"I have found that being kind and constructive when feeling self-doubt is a better choice. So, I use kind and understanding words towards myself but I also ask myself. What is one very small step I can take to move forward in this situation? Then step by step I move in that direction I want to go. Beating yourself up, is a no win for you. For me, beating myself up has only kept me in the moment of not healing. Going to sleep with it on my mind, waking up with it on my mind, eating, working out, driving, just all and any activity I would do. There was no gain to me constantly beating myself up over a situation that didn't work out the way I thought it would. There is no joy in belittling yourself. What do we gain internally by casting doubt on us, on you. What do you gain by destroying your own self esteem? Look, we are unperfect creatures. We will never get it right. Take the time, in whatever situation and be kind to yourself. Love on yourself. The world will beat us up enough, so we don't need us to be us up anymore. Self-love is the best love.

I like this because if you don't encourage yourself at times, who will? There is a gospel song by Donald Lawrence that says, "Sometimes you must encourage yourself, sometimes you have to speak victory over yourself. Sometimes you have to encourage yourself in the Lord." We all need it sometimes, and if you don't have that support system, then do it yourself. Be your biggest cheerleader. Be the one that raises your on hand for victory. Be the one that loves you harder than anyone else can ever fathom to love. I mean it is true, If you can't love yourself, how can you love someone else.

12. Celebrate that small step and win.

"It may be a small one but it's still a win. So, celebrate."

Let me ask you a question— who the hell decided what your win looks like? Who the hell told you that what you are using to measure a win isn't deep enough? Who told you that your win had to have a dollar amount tied to it. Who told you that if you didn't get so many likes on your well thought out social media post, that it was whack. People are so quick to put restrictions of winning on others, that we quickly internalize that and see ourselves as not good enough to win. I had to learn that I decide what my win and finish line look like. I decide on what small steps I celebrate. I think that part of our issues at times and why we get so discouraged is because we create these huge gaps for our victories, and when we can't reach them based on some unrealistic expectations, we get down on ourselves. And guess what? Self-doubt creeps in. A step is a foot, and to make any progress, you must take one step at a time. If you want to celebrate each step, then celebrate each step. Then celebrate the next two steps, the next four steps, and so on. My point is for you to make your own finish line. Make your victory one where you can see growth and abundance. Remember this is your life, and your life only. Some people don't want you to celebrate because they are jealous, and what we call a HATA! But let them hate, and you celebrate.

#Mindset

This is you having a #BeliefMindset. Believe in yourself; believe in your plan; believe that you can do all things through Christ who strengthens you.

13. Remember: you can course-correct along the way.

"Trying to plan every move you will make on journey towards a goal or dream can become draining and lead to quite a bit of self-doubt." This is your journey. You can develop a #BeliefMindset. Life doesn't come with a blueprint to get us from point A to point B without any difficulties or hard times and doesn't come with a recipe for cooking up the right amount of good times in our lives to keep us safe from failure. No, we must believe that we are more than our circumstances—that as we live and learn, our paths can change, and life is quite fluid. The author of your life is you, and you have the power to write in your own auto-correct. You know, one of the most annoying things is how you can type into your phone and the phone tries to outsmart you and auto correct what it thinks you mean? This can be quite frustrating, can't it? But have you taken control over your phone settings and changed what words are in the phone's power to change through auto-correct? Well, you have the same power in your life and mindset. We have the power as the author of our story to change what we can auto-correct along this action called living a life. We have the power to auto-correct negativity into positivity, anxiety into calm, mistakes into new beginnings, and fears into courage. We have that power. Change the settings in your mind to auto-correct disbelief into a #BeliefMindset. Auto-correct self-doubt into "I can achieve." Auto-correct a lazy mindset into an industrious one. Auto-correct a failing mindset into one of success and achievement.

We cannot move forward with the old thinking that kept us stuck in the muddy seasons of our lives. Break free of those habits, thought patterns, actions, and moments when you doubted yourself and all the great things God said you could have, because we are more than conquerors.

"Belief in yourself is one of the greatest tools you can develop."

#BeliefMindset

CHAPTER 2
#SURVIVORMINDSET

What is a survivor? According to the dictionary, "A survivor is a person who survives, especially a person remaining alive after an event in which others have died, also a person who copes well with difficulties in their life."

To be pushed into a place where you feel like it's life or death, you or me, my submission or my power is a place I felt many orders of the #SurvivorMindset merchandise were deriving from—people feeling like if they didn't take a stand, change their expectation, and remembered who they were, they would have died either a physical or mental death. One instance comes to mind when I delivered a hoodie to a customer in a crowded shopping mall. It was a #SurvivorMindset hoodie with a purple ribbon. I had no clue about all the color ribbons before the brand was born, but I will share more about those later in this chapter. We found each other in the busy parking lot with cars zooming by, parents trying to corral their kids, and busy walkers trying to get around us to get into the stores. I pulled the hoodie out of the bag to show her for approval. She looked at it, rubbed the ribbon, and started to cry. She was sobbing so hard that she couldn't seem to gather herself enough to tell me whether she liked it or not. I, not understanding what was happening, asked her, "Is it okay? I can re-make this ASAP!"

#Mindset

She looked at me and then the hoodie and said, "You have no idea what this means to me. I am a domestic violence survivor, and now I am advocating to help other survivors." I was floored. I began to tear up as she told me about her mindset in breaking away from such an experience—one that almost cost her, her life. Here we were in this huge parking lot, and it seemed the world had just stopped for us two. As she testified and I listened and sympathized with her situation, her testimony of realizing she was more than what was going on in her life gave me strength. We were two strangers sharing such an emotional moment—a moment of survival, resilience, power, strength, freedom, hope, and clarity. At the end of the conversation, she hugged me and thanked me for the shield on her chest. I was so blessed knowing that something I was doing at this time was making a difference to people.

You ever had that feeling or confirmation that you're doing something bigger than you and the blessing you just received was more than monetary? Later that night, I replayed our conversation in my head. There was one thing she said toward the end of the conversation that stuck out to me the most. What did she mean by the "shield on her chest"? Why did she get emotional when she first saw the hoodie and shake while she rubbed her hand on the ribbon? We all know a shield to be a source of protection, something hard and robust to keep us safe from danger. One of my favorite movies is *Troy* with Brad Pitt. In the movie, Brad Pitt plays the character of Achilles, a fierce warrior. The way he would dance the two-step while fighting any size foe was intimidating for any man to watch. When he would fight, he would twirl his shield to fend off his opponent's attack, warding off any arrows or swords coming his way. He was so skilled, it was enough to make Captain America jealous! So, what does this have to do with the shield on the hoodie? I'm glad you asked. I want to reference the following passage in the Bible that speaks of the shield of protection: "The God of my rock: in him will I trust: he is my shield and the horn of my salvation. My high tower, and my refuge, my savior, you save me from violence" (2 Sam. 22:3).

Another passage is Ephesians 6:10-18, which discusses the armor or God as discussed in Ephesians 6:10-18, but I am just going to focus on verses 14-16. "Stand firm then, with the belt of truth buckled around your waist, with the breastplate of righteousness in place, (15) and with your feet fitted with the readiness that comes from the gospel of peace. (16) in addition to all this, take up the shield of faith, with which you can extinguish all the flaming arrows of the evil one."

This lady, whom I had just met, found the shield on the hoodie to be a resemblance of what she drew her strength and power from. I obviously don't know what this woman's point of no return was, but I can only imagine her weeping at night and sobbing in the morning as she questioned why love has to hurt. I can only imagine as she absorbed each moment, both physical and emotional—the feelings of loneliness, defeat, weakness, and inferiority. I can only imagine how hard it is to feel strong and confident when you're holding in your strength to protect the actions of the weakest and worst person you know—holding in his accountability while he seeks to destroy your willingness to live. The shield that the Lord references is our protector, faith, and refuge that can save us from violence. Maybe when she rubbed that shield on the front of the hoodie, she remembered all that it took to regain her strength and escape that situation. Maybe when she rubbed that shield, she remembered who she was and not who he tried to break her into. I don't know what created the survivor mindset in this young woman's life, but I am thankful she found her power and strength.

This example of #SurvivorMindset is just one example of customers who took time out of their schedules to tell me their testimony of what a particular ribbon means to them.

#Mindset

In researching the purple ribbon of domestic violence, I remind you that domestic violence can also involve children, parents, or the elderly and can happen in a number of forms, including physical, verbal, emotional, economic, religious, reproductive, and sexual abuse. Just researching this stuff gave me eerie feelings about the things people deal with behind closed doors and then smile in public like everything is okay. It is so sad and disturbing. I pray that if you are in a situation of domestic violence, you seek help and a safe place. I can only imagine the courage it takes to walk out that door, knowing you have had enough. You are not a punching bag or a sounding board for abusive language, you are not another man's get off to make him feel masculine. It is heartbreaking to hear these stories of abuse, both physical and mental, and rape. I pray for your situation.

I remember looking at a video one night of a young lady, face black, blue, and red from her abuser. She was on the phone after the attack pretending to order a pizza to feed her oppressor in between the beating. She told the operator on the phone that she wanted a pizza, and the person on the other end of the phone said, "Ma'am, this is 9-1-1. Did you mean to call us?"

The young lady continued to order her pizza in a calm and non-emotional tone and said, "Yes, and can I add meat and sausage to the order please?"

The 9-1-1 operator now understood what was going on and asked the young lady, "Can you stay on the phone, ma'am?"

The young lady said, "No, but please hurry." I share this for anyone reading the book who might know someone in this situation so you can share this strategy with them.

#survivormindset

Love does not hurt. Love should not be an emotional earthquake that shakes your belief in yourself and causes you to always feel defeated and unworthy, and your will to even exist.

A study from National Coalition Against Domestic Violence reported that 1 in 4 women and 1 in 9 men experience severe intimate partner physical violence, intimate partner sexual violence, and /or intimate partner stalking. You can find more information on their page WWW.ncadv.org/statistics. There are also a lot of self-help groups on social media platforms for domestic violence survivors. Some of these groups and/or pages gave me life just looking at their posts and finding out some vital information.

If you are experiencing domestic violence, I just want to remind you that you are the head and not the tail. You are a Queen; you are worthy; you are not what a small-minded man yells at you to demoralize you. You are not meant to be used or abused. God did not make you for man to put his hands on you, to limit your growth, to talk to you like you don't have a heartbeat or soul. You are more than a conqueror, you are favored of the Lord, and you can make it. You can get out of that situation; the strength is within you. It may be dormant, and you may lack the confidence at this time to resurrect it, but you have the strength to rise and the power to change this outcome. I pray peace for you as I write this chapter.

I want to share with you this song by Beyoncé from when she was part of the music group Destiny's Child. The song is called "Survivor," and I want to quote part of it because the lyrics give life and hope.

> Thought I couldn't breathe without you I'm inhaling,
> You thought I couldn't see without you..perfect vision
> You thought I couldn't last without you..but I'm lasting
> You thought I would die without you..but I'm living

#Mindset

You thought I would fail without you..but I'm on top
Thought it would be over by now..but it won't stop
Thought that I would self destruct..but I'm still here
Even in my years to come..I'm still gon be here.

My sister, I pray for you right now, that as you go through your healing process from this scar, you find your strength and remember that you are favored of God. I pray that your story will be your testimony one day. You will defeat your enemy. You will be blessed, you will make it through, and you will survive. Keep giving God the glory as you think about your story, and as you gain your strength day by day, I pray that your scars will heal and you will be able to reset your life and live in prosperity.

Clap for yourself!

Being a survivor takes a strong mindset. It doesn't matter what you survive—breast cancer (pink ribbon), prostate cancer (baby blue ribbon), heart disease (red ribbon), kidney/leukemia (orange ribbon)—you made a decision to fight, just like when you had to fight through the depression from dealing with the grief of losing that job, home, significant other, child, all the stages of grief and mourning that come with a season of loss. Somewhere along the line, you had to make the conscious decision that enough was enough. I am going to fight; I can beat cancer; I can make it through chemo; I can beat heart disease; I can change my lifestyle; I can get over this grief; I can get over not having you in my life; I can get a new car; I can get a new home; I can get a new job; I can restore my credit, I can still start that business; I can still finish school; I can write a book; I can, I can, I can. Why? Because I am a survivor, and I can do all things through Christ who strengthens me.

Being a survivor takes the will of a lion. It's going to require you to reach deep down in some areas of your life and accept the challenge that is before you. Overcoming obstacles in any form isn't easy. Changing our mindset to fight, be strong, and believe we can win is not an overnight process at times. I fully understand that. But we have to train the mind to be strong, just like we have to train our bodies in the gym. Surviving is a fight, a fight we have to be willing to engage in both mentally and physically. When I made the decision in my life to seek help for me to understand my depression, I made it for me ultimately. I first thought I would do it to show my then-spouse that I was trying to change and was willing to be better. But after a few sessions, I realized I had to make that decision for me, for Derron. I pray for you to do the same. There is a song I love called "You Will Win" by Jekalyn Carr. In it she says, "It's your winning season, and you will win, lay your hand over yourself, lay hands on your mind, unleash that champion in you. You will win."

One more note:

You have to think positively, and you can't be afraid to have bad days. It's not going to be easy. It's probably going to be the hardest and most terrifying thing you will ever do. I am talking about making the decision to fight. That is why you thinking positively will train your mind to see and process things differently. As the Bible says, "Be ye transformed by the renewing of your mind." Not being afraid to have bad days is you knowing that tomorrow or the next day has the potential to be better than yesterday. It's you allowing your feelings to process and understanding that you're not perfect. You will bleed when cut, you will cry when hurt, you will be sore when rehabbing, and you will be protective when rebuilding, but you are strong and will make it through this season.

Why? Because it is your winning season, and you will win!

#SurvivorMindset – Fight to survive, fight to win, and fight to live for you are a conqueror.

CHAPTER 3

#INSPIREDMINDSET

Today was one of those days when I didn't feel inspired to write anything. I tried and tried to motivate myself, but it just wasn't happening. All of a sudden, I started having thoughts about quitting this book. I was feeling sick, I didn't have an appetite, and I was feeling a sense of self-doubt that I hadn't felt in such a long time. I knew my mind was just cluttered with junk, so I managed to roll out of bed and put on my gospel playlist to help me break out of this funk. I was feeling down about some things, and I couldn't quite understand why. It was like my mind was harassing me to be nonproductive—to stay in bed, turn on the TV, watch Netflix (probably the same show over and over), take a nap, wake up to go to work, and then do it all over again. But I told my mind, "No! I am fighting you today for ownership of my actions." See, I am still in training mode with myself. Yes, I know I am talking about mindset and trying to encourage you and inspire you to be the best you can be, but this is also a journey for me. I am writing about this subject of mindset because it's a passion of mine in this new season. But I am still learning how to develop my mind as well and teach it to be more productive, learning how to filter the pollution, negativity, and timidity out and to strengthen this muscle in my brain so I can defeat my biggest enemy, which is procrastination of the soul. Training my mind is not going to be accomplished in this short book, and neither will yours. This is a fifteen-round heavyweight fight. Boxers don't sign up for a fight then the next day hop on a plane and just show up to fight their opponent with hopes of winning. No, they train for months. They put their bodies through so much agony and pain because when it's fight time, they know they will experience so much abuse on their bodies—head punches, body punches, leg kicks, if you're into the UFC, you know what I am talking about. But At the end of the fight, they hope to be victorious, but it's a fight. That is the same with us. We can't expect to walk into a new season with an old-season mentality and ways. We can't expect to win the fight in our minds with no proper training and without giving our minds something new to focus on. I don't care what it is or who you are—you have to train. If your mind has been conditioned to failure, defeat, quitting easily, and giving power to those things that do you no good, then you are not ready for a fight. You and I have got to start training our minds to be able to compete against our inner selves. Sometimes you are the person you need to fight most. As mentioned earlier, the Bible says in Romans 12:2, "Be ye transformed by the renewing of your mind." Call me nuts, but it sounds like God gave us permission to transform our minds, to change and be better—to transform our minds from a losing #mindset to a winning #mindset, from always thinking "I can't" to believing "I can." There is power within us that is waiting to be discovered once we commit to the transformation.

So back to what was troubling me in the beginning part of this chapter. I decided to ride my bicycle one evening because I wanted to give myself a chance to think about what was troubling my mind and meditate on new thoughts and visions. The longer I rode and meditated, the more my mind began to clear up, and this chapter started to write itself. So, what was it that was creating a temporary blockage in my mind? To be honest, it was fear that came out of nowhere. I mean, I had had thoughts of uncertainty and self-doubt while writing this book but not like the fear I was feeling that day. Suddenly, my past became an issue for me, and I hadn't let that happen to me in years. All of a sudden, I started to recall all the crazy things I had done as a youth and a man. My mind was telling me, "Hey, you, are you sure you want to publish this book? Are you sure you are ready for any public scrutiny you may get? You don't want to deal with all that judgment on your character, do you? You don't really want to inspire others that much, do you? Let's just cancel the project." This is what my mind was telling me! But not this time—this time, I was going to win the battle in my mind. I was standing firm and fighting back.

I don't know what struggles you may be experiencing with your mindset, if any, but I challenge you to question yourself when you begin to plant seeds of self-doubt in your mind. Remember that you don't have to believe everything your mind says about you. You still are in control. I had felt like I was at the finish line of this book. I had handled all distractions up to this point with prayer and just being still. But now, the enemy was trying to fill my mind with thoughts of giving up and throwing in the towel. How many times in your life have you been right there at the finish line of your accomplishment, dream, or plan, and out of nowhere, that thought of throwing in the towel comes at you strong? Just think—if I had not been in the training mode of renewing my mind, I probably would have quit. We are always a decision away from walking into a fruitful season or one thought away from staying right where we are and missing out on being a blessing.

So, what was my inner battle? One of my favorite movies is *8 Mile*. In the movie, rap battles on stage in a dark, gloomy-looking warehouse were where characters' street credibility was born or died. In the early part of the movie, Eminem was in a battle with a rapper called Tic Toc. Tic Toc abused Eminem so bad on the mike, in the first rap battle, that when it was Eminem's turn to rap back against his competition, he froze. He just stood there. He was then laughed off the stage and called all sorts of vulgar names. At the end of the movie, the rap stage was set for the final battle. Eminem had just destroyed Tic Toc and was now set to battle the leader of the free world, Pop a Doc. Before the battle, one of Eminem's boys asked him in sort of a prophetic way, "Are you afraid of what he might he say?" Eminem responded, "What do you mean?" The friend said, "Well, about them sleeping with your girl, beating you up, and blacking your eye?" Eminem just stared at him, as if to say, "Man, do I really want to go through this?" Well, this was exactly how I was feeling. At that moment, I felt just like Em. *What are others are going to say? Will anyone even buy the book? Will they doubt my honesty? Will they laugh at me?* I was having a self-doubt anxiety party.

So, the rap battle in the movie was set—Eminem against the leader of the free world, the champion Papa Doc. Papa Doc was known to destroy people on and off the stage, so this battle was crucial for Em's street cred and respect. This time, Em got the mike first and hit Papa Doc with a biography of his own life. He broke down lyrically what he had been through, how his girlfriend had betrayed him with the Free World Crew, how he was living in a trailer home, and how the Free world Crew had beat him up, and how he was trailer trash. Eminem exposed himself openly, and in doing so, he released the negative energy surrounding him. He found his freedom in his own testimony by talking about his living conditions, social status, friends, and love life. Although the crowd chuckled and laughed out loud at Em, it was okay with him because he'd been freed to be himself, and the crowd was rewarding Em with cheers and praise, and hands waiving back and forth. Afterward, he gave Clarence the mic and said, "Now tell these people something they don't know about me." Papa Doc, just stood there, with nothing to say, and was eventually booed of stage.

Well, this was the trick the enemy was trying to play on me, but I was not going to drop the mic and be laughed off the stage and say to myself, "Well, maybe in 2021 I'll try again." Nah, so you know what— here is my Eminem moment. My name is Derron. I got really good parents. I went to Central High School and then went to college and dropped out. I dropped out during my second year of school because I chose to sell drugs and chase easy and fast money. About a year later, I was arrested for trafficking, then arrested a second time for DUI, then arrested a third time for shoplifting. I can remember the judge telling me when I came out from the jail cell after my third arrest to sit under the clock. Now, if you ever hear a judge in a courtroom say to sit under the clock, you know you are getting time. I heard my mother cry out my name, but I refused to look at her. The judge told me that if I came back to his courtroom one more time, he was going to give me the time on my clock, which was five years. The judge told me, "Son, get your mind right. I can tell this is not the life for you." Read that again—the judge told me to get my mind right. A man who didn't know me from any other male looked at me, saw something, and spoke a difference in my life, He let me out, and I ain't never looked back since. Oh, wait—I am not finished. I am divorced. I was not the best husband, and I cheated on my wife. I was not always the best father, son, or friend at times either, and trust me, I've made plenty of mistakes.

So, there you have it. I have just freed myself of the negative energy and hurdles to writing this book. Yes, I still have self-doubt, but I am learning to put those thoughts into perspective and understand what is driving those feeling when they show up in my mind demanding my attention. You have a story too. It may not be like mine, but you have one. Is there something in your past that is holding you back? Is there something that makes you scared to take that next step into your season? What is it that makes you doubt yourself? Are there mornings when you wake up, look in the mirror, and see something besides a Queen or King ready to conquer the world? Let me tell you—fight the enemy for control of your mind. Don't let him win anymore. Take control and make it a fight. You may lose a round or two, but keep training, keep throwing your punches, and keep listening to the trainer in your corner, which is God. And then when you least expect it, the thing that is holding you back, fighting you from within—you will throw a haymaker and catch that stronghold right on the jaw, and just like that, the fight will be over, and you will be victorious. Each Victory will make you stronger for the next.

Clap for yourself!

I want to see everyone win. It's my prayer that we all reach our fullest potential. I believe that we all have greatness inside of us and that the prayers of the righteous does availeth much. I have prayed for my girls, and I know their mom has as well, that their lives will be blessed with abundance. The same with you. I am sure that someone has prayed for your path, a prayer that protects you from some of the same mistakes they've made. Someone has prayed that you won't experience their battles, scars, losses, and pain. Someone in your family is praying that the yoke in your life be broken and that you soar like the eagles. I heard Pastor Shull say, "If generational curses can be passed down, then so can healing." It may not be an easy road. Heck, even the butterfly crawled as a caterpillar before it blossomed into something beautiful. So why can't we? Why can't you achieve your dream? Why can't you start that business? Why can't you work in the field of your passion? What is it that keeps you up all night long planning? You already have the vision—just do it. Why can't you write the book? You have the story. Just open your heart, reset your mind, and write. The famous singer Jill Scott said, "There are a lot of writers holding on to stuff because they don't know how people will accept it. And it doesn't matter. You have to get it out. You're just holding on to something that doesn't belong to you anymore." You want to save your marriage? You want to go to rehab to fight that addiction, do it, you want to go back to school, do it. There is a reason why Nike has the best slogan in the world, "Just do it" Put aside your ego and insecurities and humble yourself. To someone out there, you are an inspiration, and you don't even know it—trust me. During the course of writing this book, I was getting support from men and women who I knew and some I didn't. They didn't know I was writing a book because I kept this circle of information small. People were inboxing me and saying how much I'd inspired them. I wasn't posting anything too extravagant, just a motivational quote here and there and a workout video, but it was meeting people where they were, and it was motivation for some at the right time. This is where I give God the glory because I had no clue I had anything that would inspire people. So, thank you, God, for that energy.

As I was writing this chapter, my youngest daughter Jazlyn called me on my cell. Jaz, as we call her, shared that she was graduating from college with honors and then heading to grad school. Besides extending mine and her mom's retirement a few years to help pay for it, I was very, very, proud and happy for her new season. I told Jaz how she inspires me when I find myself in a difficult situation and that at times when my life is in turmoil, I think back to some of the trials she has faced in her young life and how with her support system, she has navigated her way through them. I took the time to tell her how proud I was of her and to encourage her to always continue to believe in herself and trust the Lord and that the battle scars the Lord has healed her from will one day be healing to someone else who reads her story. She has a book coming out soon, so I won't tell her story.

As mentioned earlier, I have two daughters. I tell Wes, my older daughter, that she saved my life, and I tell Jaz that she gave me life. When Wes came along, I was so far in the streets, and my mom told me one day, "Dee, you have got to change, or you're going to raise this child from behind bars." When I would look at Wes as an infant, she was so darn cute, and I knew I owed her my best life. I did not want to be an incarcerated dad. So I began to shift my focus to being the best father I could be for her. Then when Jaz came along, she was so active, smart, and athletic, I had to wake up my old bones just to keep up with her. These two women are an inspiration to me. Who inspires you and makes you want to be better? Who can you look at in your life and say, "Because of you, I can do this?" Who makes you want to live and achieve everything you are capable of? Sometimes the decisions we make are not for us but for those in our camps and our families. Good decisions and bad decisions can shape our loved ones. Choose wisely.

If we don't want to keep getting the same results and staying where we are, we must change our patterns. The patterns we create influence our #mindset. What we feed our minds and focus on is what we will become. You know the saying, "You won't change anything until you get mad"? Well, we can change all that before we get mad because for some of us, by the time we get mad, it's too late. I am learning to change my focus on some things and not give them power. When we focus on wrong things, things that consume our identity and don't birth growth within us, we lose power. If we can learn to change our pattern of thinking and train our minds to have a different #mindset, we can win. Did you hear me? I said, we can win!

Clap for yourself!

In this decade of 2020, I am making up my mind to do more than just exist. I want to live. I want to make a difference while I am still here. Life isn't guaranteed until you reach the age of seventy-five and over anymore. If you're fortunate, maybe you can make it to that age. TD Jakes said in a sermon, "I would hate to die before I do what I was born to do," and at this point in my life, my season, this is where I am. We all have a purpose, something that God put within us to achieve, accomplish, and give Him the glory. I don't want to die until I accomplish His will for me. Myles Monroe said, "Whatever you're born to do, is not ahead of you, it's within you." I have a gift, and you have a gift. We are more than working forty hours a week, hanging out with friends, partying every weekend, or being glued to social media for hours at a time. We are more than that. You have a vision, and you can change your altitude if you can change your attitude. The Bible says in Proverbs 29:18, "Where there is no vision the people perish." It's never too late to start to achieve that greatness in your life. Some of us mature like an old tree. It takes us 20-30 years for us to reach our potential. But that's okay—it just means our roots are firmly planted in the soil of our testimonies, and our branches are ready to give life and covering to others.

We all need some motivation and inspiration at times in our lives as we transition from season to season. I have heard it say that the Lord can't bless a closed hand, just as a closed hand can't be a blessing to someone else if it's closed. Likewise, if you have a closed mindset that feels like there is nothing it can absorb or be motivated and inspired by to grow, learn, birth new opportunities, see old possibilities as if they are new, and receive from people who can pour into you for the greater, you won't have a mindset that can motivate or inspire. What a tragedy. We all have something that we can use to inspire or motivate. Maybe it's not a book or a play you can write, and maybe it's not a social media post that can touch the right person. But it could be something as special as going to the Boys and Girls club and mentoring a youth or maybe volunteering your time at a local school. All these avenues can inspire others as well, and most importantly, our youth.

Clap for yourself!

#Mindset

As I close this chapter, it's my hope and prayer that something within these pages will speak to your heart. I tried to give you mine, and in doing so, I was able to find myself again, and for that, I thank you. I thank you because writing this book allowed me to deal with the shame of my past—the depression of my failed marriage, the lack of trust that I felt from my daughters as our home was broken up. I thank you because writing this book allowed me to take back my power from the enemy. The Bible says he walks the earth seeking to devour. But this process allowed me to pray, cry, and find peace and some encouragement as I continue to build up my #mindset. I pray that God blesses you and enlarges your territory of faith, strength, love, peace, joy, understanding, happiness, power, freedom, and increase.

#InspireMindset

CHAPTER 4
#GODMINDSET

When I started to write this chapter, this was not the topic I had studied or planned to discuss. I had planned for days to write about #VirtuousMindset.

The morning started off normal. I rolled out of bed, put my feet on the floor, and began to thank God for the day. I started thanking God for life, for forgiving me, for keeping me, and for loving me without judgement. I asked Him to be a hedge of protection around my girls, my family, my extended family, my Pastor, and my friends. I then put on my gospel playlist as I started to shave my head. The very first song on was "Rain on Us" by Earnest Pugh. The lyrics literally started to set a fire in my soul. "Let your Glory fill this place, let your all-consuming fire fill this tabernacle." Then he sings, "Purify our hearts, want you to breathe new life within us, send a refreshing glory." I couldn't contain my emotions while I was shaving my head. I began to think and reflect on how good God has been to me. Have you ever been in that situation, where all of a sudden, you're overcome with the Spirit of the Lord? Your mind starts to think of how He kept you, how He brought you out of one storm and then another, how He protected you and shielded you from your enemies and sometimes even you. Here we are in the midst of a pandemic, a literal pausing of the earth. We are encouraged to stay in our homes to stay safe and prevent the spreading of a virus that is killing people, both young and old. We are urged to only go out for essential needs and then to return to our homes. We have learned in the last month or so that some of the things we had considered essential are not. But let me stop here and say thank you to the front-line workers who have worked countless hours to help people who've contracted this deadly virus. Thank you to the nurses and other healthcare workers who nursed the sick back to health. Thank you for putting yourself and your families in harm's way.

Clap for yourself!

Now here we are, in a state of pause in our lives, and this is a perfect time for God to send a refresher in our souls. This is the time for us to find some rest, some peace, and some calmness, to reconnect with some things and discard others. This particular morning, I said I wasn't going to get on social media before I started writing, but I did, and one of my best friends, Khris, had just posted this to his Facebook page: "Time has a way of showing us what really matters in life." Ain't that the truth. We have literally just learned what we can and can't live with or without. We are learning what is important and what is not in our daily lives. With #GodMindset, I fell in love because it was a bold statement and a testimony to wear a #GodMindset across your chest. To tell anyone and everyone known and unknown that you have a #GodMindset is a declaration that you have faith that God is the author of your life. God is still in control, no matter how dim it may look. We know that God is everything and everywhere. When we understand this, then we know that God cannot fail—that He is able, that He keeps His promises, and that He loves us and will not forsake us. In the midst of many things we deal with in our lives, having a #GodMindset is a declaration that God has the power to move in our lives, deliver us from evil, and restore upon us His unmerited favor and grace. When we have a #GodMindset, we know that God is Alpha and Omega, Prince of our Peace,

Deliverer, and our Burden-bearer. We know that God loves us and wants nothing but the best for our lives.

Now there have been days in my life, as I'm sure there have been in yours, when I have wanted to just give up—to just throw in the towel and stop praying, letting whatever happens happen because sometimes the weight is so heavy, the tears are too salty, and you have cried so much that you feel dehydrated in your soul. Sometimes you have so many fears because you cannot see what God is doing in your life, and you don t know what direction you are headed in. You feel lost and alone, and you start to feel like God has abandoned you. When you call out to the Lord, you're not even sure if He hears you as you cry, "Lord, do You even care about what I'm going through? I am sad and confused about what to do. I am tired of hurting and feeling defeated. But here is where your faith steps in and the Spirit of the Lord sends you a gentle reminder that you have a #GodMindset—that He never left you and that even in the small silent moans you make, God hears them like the sound a blowing horn. He made us, and He knows how much we can bear.

Clap for yourself!

Having a #GodMindset means you trust God to be in control of your life. You know that in the midst of good times and bad, He will be there for you. During the times when you are at your lowest, when you feel lost like you can't make it another day, your #GodMindset and faith in God steps in, and you hear the voice and movement of the Spirit telling you, "I got you." Having that #GodMindset is declaring to God, "I trust where You are leading me. You know, Heavenly Father, what is best for me and what path to guide me down because You order my steps." Then the Lord will move so heavily in your life that when the season is over, you will look back at the test and praise God because He brought you through something you thought was going to take you out. All you'll know is that the Lord has blessed you and that the overflow in your life will be running over. Like Tasha Cobb Leonard said, "I'm getting ready." Get ready for that overflow; get ready for that blessing; get ready for that new season of growth and prosperity. When we develop that #GodMindset, we know that trouble won't stop. It doesn't guarantee us a life without hardships and disappointments and does not exclude us from strife, sadness, temptations, and other woes of this world. But having that #GodMindset will allow us to remember who is in control of our lives and whose we are. It will give us that reminder that the storms will soon be over and that there will be a brighter day. You know you can make it through because greater is He that is within us than he that is in the world.

What is the mindset of God? In the publication Bible.org, there is an article entitled "The Mind of God." An unknown writer wrote, "This book is the mind of God, the way of salvation, the doom of sinners, and the happiness of believers. It's doctrines are holy, it's precepts are binding; its histories are true, and its decisions are immutable."

In the Bible, there are some verses that speak directly to our mindset:

Colossians 3:2: "Set your minds on things that are above, not on things that are on earth."

Romans 8:5-8: "For those who live according to the flesh set their minds on the things of the flesh, but those who live according to the spirit set their minds on the things of the spirit. For to set the mind on the flesh is death, but to set the mind on the spirit is life and peace. For the mind that is set on the flesh is hostile to God, for it does not submit to Gods law; indeed, it cannot. Those who are in the flesh cannot please God."

Matthew 28:19: "Go therefore and make disciples of all nations baptizing them in the name of the Father and of the son and of the Holy spirit."

But my favorite verse and the verse responsible for the birthing of this brand is Romans 12:2, "Do not be conformed to this world, but be transformed by the renewal of your mind, that by testing you may discern what is the will of God, what is good and acceptable and perfect."

The #GodMindset is knowing that God can keep us in the midst and that He didn't have to wake us up this morning, but because He did, He gave us grace and mercy for one more day. It is the mindset that keeps us from going crazy when there is despair all around us. Having that #GodMindset is knowing and believing that God is in control of our lives, that hard times will not last forever, that things will get better, and that our test shall become our testimony and another person's strength. It is the belief that God can and will bring us through. It may not look like things can get brighter now, but God has the power to shift things in the blink of an eye. Having the #GodMindset is also knowing that God wants us to have the best in life. He wants us to be fruitful and for things to work out for our good. As He said in Jeremiah 29:11, "For I know the plans for you declares the Lord, Plans to prosper you and not to harm you, plans to give you Hope and a future." Having that mindset of God is a testimony to what God can, will, and has done in your life. Life will never be absent of trouble, strife, disappointment, sadness, fear, death, and hard times. There will still be nights when you cry all night and you doubt if you will ever see bright sunny days. But keep trusting God because He is still in control. He still breaks chains and has the power of life and death in His hands. He can still tell fear to behave, turn nights into bright days, wipe away every tear, move mountains, and save and protect. You and I both have a #GodMindet; we just have to embrace the love that God has for us. Sometimes we will get weak and we won't be able to fight anymore, but that #GodMindset will cause us to seek that quiet place, lie still in God's presence, and let our test become our testimony.

"When you have the mindset of God, you have the spirit of the almighty that loves you and wants the best for your life in faith and abundance."

#GodMindset

CHAPTER FIVE
#2020MINDSET

Where did this all begin? Well, let's say it started from wanting more in my life—knowing things had to change once I starting being honest with myself on why things were still the same. I had to start to take accountability for mistakes that I'd made. So I wanted to change up some things in my life and start to promote myself to a better me, getting a positive mindset with the way I looked at things, responded in situations, and grew from choices. So then I started the apparel company, which is meant to uplift and encourage.

I officially signed all documents to have #Mindset legal with the government this year, early 2020. That's why some of the brands will have "EST 2020" on them. I didn't give much more thought or meaning to it than that. I just thought of it as the company's birthday. Then one day, I stopped by my parents' home, and I had on my red #Mindset hoodie with the "EST 2020" across the chest. My dad stopped me as I was leaving and asked, "What does that EST 2020 mean?" I told him it meant the year the brand was born, my birth year. He said, "Nice, but do you know what else 2020 stands for?"

Me in a hurry and sensing one of his theological lessons coming on, said, "Uh no, tell me?"

He said, "2020 is a sign of perfect vision, right?"

#Mindset

I said, "Yes, and..."

Then he said, "And this is the year 2020, so in 2020, your mindset will be birthed with a clearer vision and purpose." I rushed out the door as he said that. He probably thought I was being rude, but I had to leave to write that down. Because if I would have stayed in the doorway, he would have said something else to make me forget what he had just said. You ever hear something so good you just had to write it down or speak it into the voice recorder on your phone just to retain it? It was confirmation, a sense of validation about what I was seeking to inspire in others and striving to live in 2020.

What Pops said marinated with me over the next few days. This is the year of 2020, a new decade to start with new ideas to brainstorm, new visions to plan, new circles to help you network, and new challenges to put you into a different position to win and succeed. It's a year of new relationships, friendships, and circumstances to inspire and encourage new thoughts and actions and a year of new territory for the Lord to enlarge. This year, let's fight against whatever held you captive in 2019. Fight that addiction, that losing mentality, that depression. Take the fight to whatever plagued you, and find your way to dream again, love again, and believe in yourself again. You can achieve; you can start that business; you can become debt-free; you can start or finish school. You just have to start. One of the biggest reasons people don't achieve their purpose is they never start. This is 2020, the year of a new, clearer vision, a clearer vision and a stronger #Mindset.

Clap for yourself!

Life will return one day after this pandemic, and although there may be a new normal, don't let this hold you back. Don't miss this year of clearer vision to not work on your growth and abundance. Hopefully there was something during this downtime that allowed you to grow in some area of your life.

I knew coming out of 2019, that I was going to have to change some things in my life—people, places, TV shows, music, habits, food...well, maybe not foods. Hey, I like to eat! But we all have to change something to move forward in our lives. We can't keep the same mentality that produced no growth, happiness, joy, or prosperity. For some of us, we may have to change our friends and our surroundings. If we don't, we will continue in a losing battle because we have developed so much dependency on others and what they think about us. Sometimes we are going to have to fight ourselves. The way we see ourselves can be a battle at times. To make changes in your life, you are going to have to lose dead weight. That's okay, because everybody can't go with you on every journey, which was a lesson I had to learn as well. And that is fine because the same applies to me—there are some journeys that my friends go on that aren't intended for me either. So, yes, some people and places you're going to have to leave right where they are because they can't go with you. They won't understand your journey or why you're trying to do or be better. To be honest, we probably should have left them in 2018 or 2017! Aren't you tired of carrying dead weight? This is your year to birth something new and believe in yourself and what you can achieve—to strive to be the best you can be and as Nike says, "Just do it."

Let me be honest here for a minute. I almost didn't write this book. Like I said earlier, I started this process two years ago, but there was so much going on in my life then that I knew I wasn't mentally ready to write it. So, at the end of last year when I started to just make little notes on my phone and in my voice recorder that I could go back and reference, I was preparing myself for this book. However, self-doubt stepped in, and I started to make every excuse why I should not write the book. *How do I start? What could I say for so many pages? What will* people think of me? Can I afford it? Who will proofread all my grammatical errors? Do I even have time? I am working seventy-plus hours, trying to act, work out, socialize, be a better son, brother, and dad, and then there is the dog I have to walk so many times a day, and what about my me time? I mean I had made every excuse I could think of not to write this book. But the burning was there, along with the vision and desire. Have you ever had a burning in your gut so strong that no matter how you ignored it, it would just burn hotter? I remember opening up to a good friend of mine, Rodney Pitts (RP). I told RP about it because I had developed a level of trust with him while I was going through my divorce. He helped me keep it together mentally and emotionally. Let me say here: "RP, thank you, bruh. I love you." Well, I told RP one day when we were on the phone, "Man, I've been thinking about writing a book."

I could hear him pause on the other end, and then he said like only he can, "Well, dammit, do it."

I chuckled and said, "But don't you want to know what it's about?"

He said, "Nope, just do it. Just like when you wanted to be an actor, I told you to just do it, and you're doing fine. So if you want to write the book, just do it. Stop doubting yourself." That meant a lot to me because he didn't want to or need to know what I wanted to share. His job at that moment was to encourage me.

I asked RP sometime later, "Why didn't you ask me what the book was about?"

He said, "You didn't need my opinion on the content; you needed my encouragement on the process." Sometimes we don't need to have all the answers to show support and encouragement. Sometimes just showing people support on the level they are at is enough to fill the spirit. Being supportive isn't always knowing the what, how, when, and where. It is also about being encouraging through the process.

Another instance:

When this pandemic hit, my mutual friend Dwight Chapmen "DJ Kaos" was DJing live on all his social media platforms, just like a lot of DJ's and entertainers were doing. But he was different. He was local and famous for being the number one and only DJ for the Great Slick Rick the Ruler. I was honored to be his friend. How many of us grew up listening to album or cassette tapes of Children's Story? It had hits like "La DI DA," "Mona Lisa," "The Ruler's Back," and so many more. Whew, I almost starting dancing, and trust me, I have no rhythm! I wanted to show support for DJ Kaos, so I made him a special Mindset shirt called #KaosMindset. I did this as appreciation for what he was doing in his free time, keeping everyone across the world at home and safe while jamming to his music. I was shocked when I tuned in to his live feed one afternoon, and he was wearing the shirt on his broadcast. I was so blessed to see that, and he even dedicated the show to his #KaosMindset shirt, saying that he drew his inspiration to do that day's show from the surprise he received in the mail, which was the shirt. A few days later, Kaos and I had a chance to connect over phone. This was our first time speaking outside of an event and over the phone. We shared a lot during that conversation, enough to where I felt comfortable in telling him I was trying to finish a book but was feeling some doubt and maybe some fear. Kaos said, "Dee, just do it. It's not your job to be perfect in your delivery; it's just your job to deliver the message that God gave you and let the message fall where it may. Your job is to be obedient and deliver it because you don't know who you're meant to inspire." That conversation that day blessed me and still continues do so.

#Mindset

So, let me recycle that for you. I believe all of us are born with greatness inside of us. And some of us right now have a passion, a dream, or a vision to put that greatness out into the world—not for the world to take notice but because it's what we've been called to do. God gave us that vision, that burning, that desire, and if we can share that somehow and some way, we never know who we might bless, ultimately giving God the glory. You want to start that business? Prepare for it and start it. You want to write that book? Then study your subject and start writing. You want to be a better man, a better woman? Then prepare your mind and your heart and do it. You want to start/finish school? Then get your mind right and do just that. Even with just living a healthier lifestyle, get in the gym, stay out the kitchen with bad foods, and just do it. Just remember while you are preparing for all these things you want to accomplish in this year and decade of 2020 to give almighty God glory and be prepared for your blessing. Remember Matthew 6:33: "But seek first his kingdom and his righteousness, and all these things will be given to you as well."

You have something that someone needs this year, this decade, and something you need to do. This year of 2020 and new decade is the beginning of your clearer vision. This is still your year to get up and say to yourself, "I am a king; I am a queen. I can do this; I can do that." See it, see it, see it. If you are lacking that 2020 vision, seek God's face, then seek out someone who can pour into you. This is what I did. I came across many individuals who inspired me to finish this project, even if they didn't know they had. It may have been in a story they told or maybe a post I read. It could be in a sermon my pastor spoke or maybe a song I heard. Inspiration can come in a multitude of ways once your mind is engaged and focused on the vision.

You can have it; you can achieve it. This is your year, your decade to change your #Mindset and trajectory. TD Jakes said it best: "There is nothing more powerful than a changed mind," and I'll add 2020 vision to that statement. Don't let fear and self-doubt keep you in isolation. Isolation from success and isolation from achieving your goals will land you in an isolation of failure. Start today, start tomorrow—just start. The only thing holding you back is you. I really didn't believe that to be true, but I really do now. You can blame everything or everybody, but the person who controls the twenty-four hours in your day is you.

God bless you and thank you for reading my book.

In this year of 2020, I pray for you to have a clearer vision of your purpose and goals for abundance.

#2020Mindset

CHAPTER 6

#FOCUSEDMINDSET

We all want to be the best. There is no kidding anyone that we don't want the worries of paying bills, living from check to check, or staying in a small place where it's just cramped. We all want the American dream to have more, be more, be financially secure, be able to acquire nice things in life, travel, and take two or more vacations every year to allow our family to see the world and gain a wealth of knowledge by observing and learning new cultures. We all want status and to be respected in the field we are in. I was just talking about Moguls a few chapters ago, and a mogul doesn't become a Mogul without being focused on something at some point in his or her career. When you were a child and people yelled, "You're not focused!" they were just trying to get the best out of you—trying to push and motivate you, attempting to reel your focus back in so you could deliver the proper results. The same applies to you today when you say the same thing to people in your life. Aren't you just trying to get the best out of them? I can remember when my oldest daughter Weslie wanted to run track. Boy, was she fast. Wes was a natural athlete at any sport. Tennis, track, basketball, gymnastics—trust me, the child was a beast! But she just lacked focus at times. It was hard to keep her on task to understand her full potential. Yes, she was good, and she knew it. She was short but powerful, so when it came to soccer, she would dribble right around the other kids with grace and speed for easy goals.

#Mindset

With gymnastics, her frame was so strong and compact that a flip was like second nature to her. Boom, done—what's next? Lol. But track and soccer—whoa, she was it. Before I understood how it really worked with high schools and coaches, I was being approached by school boosters about Wes playing for them. As I mentioned before, she was really good, but she lacked focus—not the will to play or be the best, but focus. Now, parents, pay attention to what I'm about to say. I did too! I didn't understand the power of focus in my life to help her with the focus she needed in her life. I did not know how to help her with somethings she needed in order to be the best she could be when I was lacking in it. As an untrained parent who, of course, wanted the best for his child in all areas, not just sports, I saw her lapses of play and didn't understand how to move those lapses from frustration to focusing on being better in those moments. I would just yell and fuss at her. "Come on, you can do it! Come on, you are not tired!" Now when I go to youth games and I hear parents yell that, it urks me to no end.

There is no secret formula to being focused and staying on task. We all have the innate ability to wander in our thoughts and then label it multi-tasking. We all have greatness inside of us. No one is born with the mindset of, "I want to be a failure; I want to be broke, I want to be mediocre." Nah, no one wakes up every day and says, "This is a day to go to work and be fired." I hope that none of us lives a real-life experience like in the movie *Friday*, when Chris Tucker got fired on his day off! I do believe that we all want the American dream. And I am telling you right now, you can have it, and I can too. I remember my Pastor Corrie Shull saying one sermon, "You are never too old to achieve. Start today." Let's look at some information that can help you stay focused.

In *Inc.* newsletter, there was an article titled "7 Mindsets That Will Improve Your Life Right Now."

#focusedmindset

1. Self-trust mindset

"To do anything great, you have to be able to trust yourself and believe in your capabilities. Success is not something that just happens but sometimes it's something you create. You have to have the confidence to banish any negative voices in your head. Don't give up on the things you believe in and most important, don't give up on yourself." Belief in yourself is one of the greatest tools you should learn and strengthen.

Self-trust is a must in anything. We will always have our doubters or haters, as we say. Some say if you don't have haters then you are not doing anything worth noticing. There will always be people who will not believe in you or have confidence that you can be successful. But you can't be that person to yourself. You have to stay focused on your goal. You have to find the station of your mind that only two people have the frequency to, your Almighty Savior and you. Distractions will come and go; sometimes they stay around longer than others do. Distractions can come to kill and destroy, to take us away from our mission and calling in our lives. So you have to stay focused and see things for what they are, and not be afraid to cut them out your life.

Don't stick around those people who just don't know how to support us; rather, find the support in someone who can be the positive force you need. Every now and then, I like to play the song I mentioned earlier by Donald Lawrence and the Tri City Singers called "Encourage Yourself." Speak over yourself and distance the negative thoughts and people in your life out of your circle. Besides, we know now that everybody isn't meant to go along with us on our journey. Everybody can't share your glory. We will shed people and friends like snakes shed skin. Even the butterfly once crawled before it flew.

2. Goal-setting mindset

#Mindset

"Knowing what you want and willing yourself to reach it are two different things. When you know your goals, they motivate you. Remember, if it doesn't challenge you, it won't change you. Set high goals and don't stop until you reach them."

What is it that motivates you? Is it money? Is it fame? Is it the ability to move about as you please? Is it leaving a legacy for your family? Is it being able to help your community? What is it? Those are your answers to the beginning of your "why." Whatever it is that you want, you have to be ready to face the challenge head on. It is not going to be easy. If it was, wouldn't everyone do it? We would all be millionaires, CEOs of our own companies, and have the nicest cars and the biggest homes, but we know that isn't the case. What is factual, however, is that to achieve any level of greatness, there has to be sacrifice. There will be moments when you can't hang with your crew, when you have to turn off all your devices to focus on achieving your goals, when you will have to sacrifice so much of yourself that it will require you to question, "Is it all worth it?" Long days, long nights, sleepless nights and zombie days, will be a prerequisite. What if someone told you that if you poured everything you could into yourself for the next few months to learn and develop your opportunities that it would determine your lifestyle in the next two years. Would you sell out for it? Would you be willing to make all the sacrifices you could to reach your goal? Ofcourse you would, I know I would, but success isn't coming with a gurantee.

3. Patient mindset

"There's a fine line between moving forward and standing still. The most successful people do all they can to move forward, but they also have the patience to wait and watch. Those who are impatient tend to lose out on great opportunities. Sometimes you have to wait for the right thing."

Well, you know the old saying that patience is a virtue? I know we have all heard that and had the experience of saying to ourselves, "I knew I should had waited." Waiting on what we want is hard for us, especially in this microwave society where we want everything right now to be instant. No one I know likes instant mash potatoes, they would rather wait to the made from scratch pot is done. But patience is a mindset that allows us to slow down and move meticulously. Being patient isn't about moving scared or being afraid to take an opportunity. Being patient is allowing us to check ourselves before we wreck ourselves.

4. Courageous mindset

"Doing anything great requires courage, but fear always has a way of showing up. Courage does not mean being unafraid; having and showing courage means facing your fears, saying 'I am scared and I am moving forward anyway.' Courage is like a muscle you can strengthen with use."

God didn't give us the spirit of fear. But to be fair, we all don't experience fear and anxiety in the same way. What may cause me fear or anxiety may not do the same for you. But God has the same message for us all, no matter how we handle fear and anxiety. That message is found in Philippians 4:6-7: "Do not be anxious about anything, but in every situation, by prayer and petition, with thanksgiving, present your requests to God. [7] And the peace of God, which transcends all understanding, will guard your hearts and your minds in Christ Jesus."

And about fear, the Lord tells us in 2 Timothy 1:7, "For God hath not given us the spirit of fear; but of power, and of love, and of a sound mind."

Being courageous when it is so easy to play it safe and make excuses about why you didn't do this or that takes strength.

I have made up in my mind that I don't want to be labeled a quitter anymore. I told you earlier that I have been called a quitter. That word stings me to my core, especially when it has some truth behind it. I am in this to win it now. I know there will be days and nights when I won't be my best, and that is okay because just like in any sport, anyone can lose on a given day; but the best teams, the winning teams, always find a way to get back into the action and practice harder on their weaknesses to get back on the winning track. This year and for the years to follow, as long as the Lord gives me breath, I don't want to become the consequence of me quitting before I give it my all to win.

5. Focused mindset

"One of the worst setbacks that can happen is losing focus and allowing procrastination to step in. Important as it is, it's difficult to be focused and disciplined. The best way is to stay in the here and now and to concentrate on everything going on in this particular moment. Distraction wastes time, and procrastination keeps you from moving forward. Discipline is the bridge between goals and accomplishments, and a mindset of focus builds that bridge."

Having a #FocusedMindset requires us to be present in the here and now and try to concentrate on everything going on in that particular moment. We have greatness inside of us, the power to achieve and be successful in our lives. Whether it's in your business, professional work career, school, sports, entertainment, or just in general, you have it; we all do. Learning to be focused is like anything else. We have to train ourselves to stay on task and learn how to remove our distractions. You have heard it said that an idle mind is the devils workshop. Well, it's true, isn't it? When our minds linger on things that don't bear good fruit, it opens the door for the negative in our lives to take up residence. Whether be meditating, limiting multi-tasking, working in quiet environments, eating before you work, or whatever, find what best works for you and push the best out of you to achieve your goals in life. Let's get focused on our journey to produce the best life we deserve. Greatness is within you. There is more greatness in us than self-doubt. We just have to learn to believe in ourselves more than we nurture the doubt in ourselves.

Writing this book, I had so many distractions. It was a blessing that we found ourselves in the middle of a global quarantine in a way, but the curse was I had more time than ever to manage in my day. But I made up my mind that if I didn't finish this book during these times, I probably would never finish it because I had wanted to write a book for almost two years and kept finding a way to procrastinate with something else. So, I made a list of things I had to accomplish each day. I was still required to work my hours for my job every day, but I put the other things into categories. After the list, I focused on the things that had higher importance. I remember looking in the mirror and saying, "You are about to write this book. Let's go. No more excuses." I was actually practicing being focused. When distractions came up like the cell phone, checking social media, text messages, ESPN, the dog wanting a treat, I would push the non-essential distractions to the side. Find your niche way to focus and your "why" to stay on track, and remember that once your mindset is focused, it is very powerful and dangerous.

I don't want to ever have the feeling again that if I could have just stayed focused on this or that I could had achieved this or that outcome. Being focused is a part of our minds that we have to train. If you can't stretch the capacity of your mind to stay focused, you will always be at war with distractions, and probably continue to lose. Staying on task or focused is not a strong skill set for me, I really have to mind my self in this area to produce the best result I can. I think I need medication now as an adult more than I probably did as a child. My crew teases me a lot, for if we make plans, I am all in, but they never expect me to be there until I actually show lol. I just lose focus at times, but I am getting better. Thank God!

6. Positive mindset

"Choosing to be positive and having a good attitude will determine a lot about your life. If you set your mind to positivity it can go a long way. Be positive, not passive. Instead of giving yourself reasons why you can't or shouldn't, give yourself reasons why you can and permission to go for it. Happiness doesn't come from circumstances but always from within." I had a lady who ordered a shirt that read #PositiveMindset. I asked her why she chose to tag her shirt with that, and her response was simple but profound. She said, "If I am going to invest in the two energies, one being positive and the other being negative, I would rather put all my energy into the positive so I feel better." I have to agree with that statement. I firmly believe that we are our own worst enemies at times. We allow too many factors to control what we say and how we react and feel. You don't have to always respond to ignorance or give validation to intelligence. One of my hardest lessons I have learned and am still trying to perfect is the art of walking away. I do not owe you anything, Mr. or Mrs. Negative. I have the power to choose what I will give my energy to. Enough faking it to make it. That is draining. I don't want to wear a fake smile, and I don't want you to either if you're around me. There is so much power in encouraging each other. I am a believer that iron does sharpen iron. I believe we can push each other to get better, be better, and achieve together. If it takes more energy to frown, then give me a smile all day. Are you going to let the ones who sat in the back of your life be the loudest in your life? I remember during one of my reviews with my Manager, I was praised and scored high on people development. I told my Manager that I will give a person every opportunity to be their best, to want success, to strive for more, and reach beyond their possibilities. I want people to see the positives, not just the negatives. It is so much of that already. I will push you at work, I will dang near get on your nerves, until you make me stop, because I believe in the positive.

7   Learning mindset

"Just because you are struggling, that doesn't mean you're not learning. Every failure has something to teach you, and everything you learn helps you grow. If you are unwilling to learn, no one can help you: if you are determined to learn, no one can stop you."

Every great success requires some kind of struggle, and good things really do come to those who work hard to pursue the goals and dreams they believe in. To radically change your life, you have to change yourself. Start building your new mindset today—think the thought that will help you move toward your goals right now. Dive deep into podcasts and you tube videos that are tailored to what you want to achieve. Attend seminars, zoom meetings, networks meetings, to meet new people and possibly network with more like minded individuals like yourself. I have a friend who has become more like a mentor to me, one of many, that makes close to a million dollars if not more. But before he acquired his millions he use to blow my mind with the money he would invest in himself to learn and set in the company of people or groups that had the knowledge to help him further his career. I have seen him pay upward 100k's for these sessions. I am no where near this kind of investment in myself..YET, but I hope to be one day, and I will. However, there are many levels of learning that are free, that I have began to capitalize on to enhance my knowledge on certain subjects. Progression is better than stagnation.

#FocusedMindst

CHAPTER 7
#VIRTUOUSMINDSET

The word virtuous means "having or showing high moral standards." This will probably be my most transparent part of the book. So, fellas, just bear with me in this chapter.

The Bible speaks in the book of Proverbs 31 about what it means to be a virtuous woman.

> 10 [a]A wife of noble character who can find?
> She is worth far more than rubies.
> 11 Her husband has full confidence in her
> and lacks nothing of value.
> 12 She brings him good, not harm,
> all the days of her life.
> 13 She selects wool and flax
> and works with eager hands.
> 14 She is like the merchant ships,
> bringing her food from afar.
> 15 She gets up while it is still night;
> she provides food for her family
> and portions for her female servants.
> 16 She considers a field and buys it;
> out of her earnings she plants a vineyard.
> 17 She sets about her work vigorously;
> her arms are strong for her tasks.
> 18 She sees that her trading is profitable,

and her lamp does not go out at night.
¹⁹ In her hand she holds the distaff
and grasps the spindle with her fingers.
²⁰ She opens her arms to the poor
and extends her hands to the needy.
²¹ When it snows, she has no fear for her household;
for all of them are clothed in scarlet.
²² She makes coverings for her bed;
she is clothed in fine linen and purple.
²³ Her husband is respected at the city gate,
where he takes his seat among the elders of the land.
²⁴ She makes linen garments and sells them,
and supplies the merchants with sashes.
²⁵ She is clothed with strength and dignity;
she can laugh at the days to come.
²⁶ She speaks with wisdom,
and faithful instruction is on her tongue.
²⁷ She watches over the affairs of her household
and does not eat the bread of idleness.
²⁸ Her children arise and call her blessed;
her husband also, and he praises her:
²⁹ "Many women do noble things,
but you surpass them all."
³⁰ Charm is deceptive, and beauty is fleeting;
but a woman who fears the LORD is to be praised.
³¹ Honor her for all that her hands have done,
and let her works bring her praise at the city gate.

I posted the entirety of verses 10-31 from the NIV because I think we need to be reminded of the treasure that God has placed inside of a virtuous woman. Or maybe for some us, we need to understand what we have and how we need to cherish, respect, honor, love, protect, show loyalty, and thank God for the women in our lives. For others, this chapter may be a reflection on what we've lost. The woman who we had in our grasp, our hearts, and our lives that we didn't appreciate and is now gone—a woman who was given to us that we failed as a man to show virtue to. Moment of transparency here—during my divorce, I began to see the virtue of my wife. I began to see how special she truly was and how blessed she was in the Lord and began to understand her value verse by verse. She wasn't perfect—none of us are—but she did walk with and live with virtue. I pray the best for her life now and forever.

As men, it is our job to protect our women—not to treat them like they aren't our equals or are lessor companions. Rather, we are called to respect them, to show value to, build with, love, and cherish. Men, we have got to get from the point that we can't learn from our women, that their value is not one to be respected or admired. The Lord gave them exactly what He gave us and that is the will to be great, honored, respected, loved, and cherished. It just took our crazy society a little longer to realize the preciousness in our women.

The Bible says, "Who can find a virtuous woman? For her price is far above rubies." Rubies are less common than diamonds and based on the stone, more expensive. I appreciate the woman who wears a #VirtuousMindset hoodie. She knows her worth and is coming into her own on how she wants to be treated and what she deserves. Many scars may have probably led to this moment, many tears may have soaked her pillow at night, and many heartaches and lonely nights may have been in her past and still in her present, but she is evolving. She is growing and finding her independence, will, drive, meaning, and purpose, and she is finding her worth outside of a man's charm, arms, and sense of security. Men, we got to do better with our women. We expect them to be everything to us. We want them to care for us, take care of the household and the family in our absence, have dinner ready when we get home, and have the kids homework done before we get home, but at times, we don't reciprocate the process or the energy they give us. We act like they owe that to us, like they should be proud we chose them, but in retrospect, you do remember who God called lonely, don't you? In Genesis 2:18, "Then the LORD God said, 'It is not good that the man should be alone; I will make him a helper fit for him.'" So who are we to treat our women like they need us, like we are above them? We are the ones who needed a helper.

I was listening to Alicia Keys "A Woman's Worth" one night. That song was like the theme song for women for the whole year after it was released. "You can buy me diamonds, you can buy me pearls, Take me on a cruise around the world, baby you know I'm worth it. Dinner lit by candles, run my bubble bath, make love tenderly to last, to last, cause baby you know I'm worth it." A virtuous woman is a gift from God. We have to do better by showing them respect because otherwise, they will find a man who knows their worth.

Our queens know how precious they are—first to God, then to themselves, and then to their families. It's important for a woman who to develop that self-love for herself because we all know that no matter your gender, you can't love anyone unless you love yourself first. Carolyn Cole, LCPC, LMFT, NCC said in an interview with Bustle.com, "Self-love is learning to love oneself. Just as when you think of being fully in love with a partner, you experience feelings such as unconditional love, adoration, compassion, and forgiveness – and when you experience self-love, you have these feelings about yourself! You look at yourself in the mirror and remind yourself of how amazing and adorable you are." Building up your self-love will increase the meaning of virtue in your life. You know what you have on the inside of you. You know your value and what you expect, and you know you don't have to lower your expectations for anyone. If anything, you know the demand for your value because you are set apart. You have those qualities in your mindset, and you don't have to settle for something or someone that has the potential to cause a disturbance in your peace.

With a #VirtuousMindset, you know that you are strong, independent, highly respected, considerate, and compassionate. With a #VirtuousMindset, you know you are trusted and powerful.

I asked my mom her thoughts about a virtuous woman. I mean, I have known this woman all my life and seen many of her obstacles as a kid, young man, and grown man. So, I asked her, "Mom, when did you realize your virtue as a woman?"

As she thought about it, tears welled up in her eyes, and she said, "When I was a young woman, I always wanted to be a mother and wife and have a career in nursing. But when my mom got sick, my focus changed. My journey started then for I had to learn to become a caregiver while being a wife and a mother. Sometimes the journey was painful, sad, and many other things, but God kept me. We were raised in a church and went every Sunday and sometimes throughout the week but still did not truly know or love for Jesus. Marriage was a struggle at times, like any other married couple that is young and in love. There were sometimes I couldn't find the peace I needed with so much going on and sometimes I would do without for my family to do with. Then I met a man I didn't know but knew of and fell in love on a Thursday night. His name was Jesus! His name is Jesus! He met me where I was and didn't leave. He showed me how to connect to Him, and in that, I saw my worth. A virtuous woman is a woman who loves and fears God and walks in His commands because walking in His commands and promises means I'll never fall without Him catching me. Yes, son, I am a Proverbs 31 woman, a woman with a #VirtuousMindset, who knows her worth and is not afraid to fail, live, love, trust, or die because God holds me in His hands, and I love Him, and He loves me. I recognized that my inner peace that I yearned for and deserved could not come from man on this earth or anything else. I had to seek that out for myself, and that came from God, our Father."

Clap for yourself!

Now, clap for yourself again!

Know your worth; know your value; know your peace; know your joy; know your virtue.

#VirtuousMindset

CHAPTER 8

#MOGULMINDSET

A mogul, according to the Free Dictionary, is a "very wealthy or powerful business person, a business leader, magnate, top executive, or tycoon."

Reaching the heights of being considered a mogul will be met with many challenges—challenges not just from others but from your mind as well. You have to find that part deep inside you that will block out all distractions and all individuals who will seek to keep you down. You think Beyoncé, Rihanna, Taylor Swift, Jay-Z, Diddy, Bill Gates, Oprah, Robert Smith, Jeff Bezos, Steve Jobs, and our own home Louisville, KY, resident Junior Bridgeman and countless other moguls did not have moments of doubt? You bet your bottom dollar they did! There will surely be people who will not believe in you and will let you know that you're just wasting your time. They will show you jealousy and lack of support and disregard your every move, and some will hate on you behind your back. But you can't let that distract you or delay you. This is your moment, your time. One thing that non-supporters don't see or feel is your vision. They are not there when you are having your spirit constantly disrupted with plans and ideas. They aren't there at 3:00 or 4:00 am when your brain is busy and won't let you sleep and doesn't care how tired you are the next day or week. Sleepless nights and long days should come as a prerequisite for wanting to be a mogul and be successful. The sleepless nights to make money will one day result in making money while you sleep. Being a mogul isn't for everyone. It sounds cute: "I want to be a Mogul. I want to be wealthy. I want the best money can buy. I want financial freedom," but are you really built for the struggle?

I can remember a time when I was part of an investment group. At the time, the group was looking to start a franchise. So like others in the group, I did some research on possible franchises that would have sustainability in the growing town that I was working in. The town was growing by leaps and bounds, partly because of the new production plant that had been built years ago. But what I saw was that people in the town were leaving their own area and traveling to a larger city to take care of personal business. I remember going into that little growing town hours before work and just riding around, sometimes parking in certain areas and watching people go about their daily lives. I was just trying to see what the people of the community's needs were—the trends, the patterns, the time of day when the so-called strip malls were the busiest. Then one day, it hit me—the perfect franchise. So I did my research, called the company, got the information emailed to me, and talked to the franchise department. I had all my information and was ready and excited for the next quarterly meeting with the investment group. I rolled out the plan to the group, and everything was fine. The presentation went over well. We would then meet in a month to vote. The next meeting came, and they voted against my idea of the franchise! I was in shock. So to spare you the rest of the story, a year later, a competitor came along and bought out every franchise store starting at a million dollars minimum. When I tell you I was sick to my stomach, I mean it, but it taught me a hard lesson that people don't always see your vision. That doesn't make you right or them wrong. It's just that the vision could have been just for you. I know and understand that this kind of situation had just as much opportunity to turn out the other way if we'd pursued it, but the lesson I learned for me was to bet on yourself and do your due diligence. If the numbers are right and the vision is clear, seek the opportunity, and don't give up on yourself so fast.

As you move toward your dream of being a Mogul in your industry, whether it be real estate, entertainment, technology, business, or whatever, you have to build that mindset in you that it's your vision. It is what the Lord planted in you. Being a Mogul is a passion. It's a burning that is deep inside of you, a desire to be great and be the best. It is possible to be the best and to have everything you want. But it's not going to be easy, and there are some strategies and behaviors that you are going to have to learn and develop. Belief in yourself is so important. Let's be real—can you imagine the neighborhood talk about the guy down the street with a junkie garage, making the neighborhood look bad? "Clean that up, close the door, it's a fire hazard, you're taking my property value down." I am talking about the man who has made billions from an online website. What would have happened if Jeff Bezos, the owner of Amazon, would have listened to all those people and not taken his possibilities and turned them into opportunities? We can do this. We have to learn to block out the negative and see the positives. Take advantage of the now we have and master it into the future we all want. It is there within your reach. You just have to believe in yourself to make it happen. See it; plan it; work it; achieve it; live it.

Clap for yourself here!

To be a Mogul in any field, there are some things we have to do. First of all, we have to believe in ourselves. Sometimes the things we do and the moves we make will not make sense to others, even our loved ones at times. Are you okay with standing alone to achieve that dream? I am not saying being isolated from those you care about or to discredit how they feel, but I am saying, are you built to handle those tough conversations when people don't believe in you and think you are crazy? Can you believe in yourself? What do you tell that person in the mirror to waken up the beast in you. We have to develop thick skin and an abundance mindset. I love this because the brand of #Mindset is to encourage a mindset of growth and abundance. To be a Mogul, you have to believe that you can be the best and can have it, whatever that "it" is. Don't let people who don't understand you stop you. If it was for them, the Lord would have given it to them.

I found an article that outlines five things that can hold a person back from becoming a mogul:

1. You don't set goals. You have to set your goals and follow through with them. Some people like to set micro goals to keep them inspired, others like to make larger attainable goals. Whatever your method, you will need to set some goals for achievement.
2. You don't know where your time goes. How many hours per day do you spend on your inbox? Use social media responsibly
3. You don't think long term. Don't let todays task overshadow tomorrow's successes.
4. You don't have an abundance mindset. To become a mogul, you have to think big.
5. You don't hustle. No one accidentally became a billionaire sitting around watching TV and playing video games. Taking time off is important, but you won't go far if you don't hustle.

(Eric Rosenberg).

#mogulmindset

An article published by BET in 2016, titled "10 Things You Need to Do to Be a Mogul" stated:

1. Start your own business
2. Make your money work for you
3. Establish good credit
4. Network aggressively
5. Spend smart
6. Take risks
7. Get organized
8. Know the law
9. Build a strong team
10. Visualize, write, execute

To reach the heights of being considered a mogul and have that kind of influence in the world, there is definitely a mindset that one has to have. Because it's not easy—no one is going to give you millions or status unless you inherit it.

It's a mindset. You have to be willing to wake up every morning and work all day and sleep all night with the dream. Do what it takes to make the dream into a reality. If it was easy, everyone would do it, right? But it can be done. It can be yours and is within your reach.

At work we have this saying: "What is your why?" I believe you can use the same thought pattern here. What is your why? Why do you want this? Why is this important? Why will this make yours and your loved ones' lives better? Why should you continue on and not quit? Okay, good—now that you got those whys answered, let's get to work! Look, opportunities are like the wind. They will blow past you if you're not ready.

You want to live your best life? Well, living our best lives doesn't end with a dream but starts with the execution of a vision.

#Mindset

When it gets hard (and it surely will) and fear creeps into your mind, just remember to focus on the value you will be adding.

I asked Chea Woolfolk, whom I have grown to admire and respect for her hard work and determination in her efforts to bring forth positive news and entertainment via her media companies, to shed some light on what she thought it meant to be mogul.

"What does it mean to be a mogul?

This is a layered question yet; I have a simplified view on the topic.

For me, being a mogul means building something that provides opportunities for others. By creating platforms that allow others to share their talents, we can achieve global impact.

I feel that we all deserve to be heard, and my goal has been to provide opportunities for that to occur. I know that in the entertainment industry, the word "mogul" causes many to think of fancy parties, videos, and red carpets.

For me, the word "mogul" means granting as many entrances into the industry as possible—scouting talent and giving them the microphone, reading manuscripts and giving them a printing avenue, hearing comedians and granting them a stage. And so on and so on until we have given the world a glimpse into the hidden talents of our generations.

Mogul does not mean, "I know it all." It just means, "I am willing to learn as much as I can to achieve my goals." My inspiration and unofficial mentor is Clarence Avant. This man has literally touched every part of entertainment and beyond. He moved in silence but gave his knowledge without trying to overshadow the artists, creatives, and talent. He brought people together who needed each other to achieve a vision, and he did so selflessly, educating those new to the industry on how to create their empires while building others up.

My philosophy is, 'The more people I put on the more my territory and reach grow'" (Chea K. Woolfolk).

#MogulMindset

THE END

Again, I would like to thank you for taking this journey with me. It means a lot that you took the time out of your busy schedules to walk with me page by page. This was not an easy project. It was demanding, lonely, and confrontational within my soul at times, but with the help of God, I made it through. I pray that whatever your dreams and visions are, you continue to push forward and achieve them. I am already researching and learning new material for my next project, so please be patient with me as I learn daily on how to be the best version of myself so God can use me. I am a work in progress, but just as that new construction looks different week to week, so will the foundation of my journey until I am where God wants me to be. Again, thank you and be blessed.

BOOK REFERENCES:

survivormindset
Ephesians 6:10-18

Beyoncé song called I'm a survivor (released in 2002) written by Beyoncé Knowles, Anthony Dent, Matthew Knowles.

Jekalyn Carr song called "You will win"
(Released in 2018. Written by Jekalyn Carr
William McDowell Song called "I Give Myself Away" written by William McDowell
Inc Newsletter article "7 Mindsets that will improve your life right now"
Donald Lawrence and the Tri City singers. "Encourage yourself"
Philippians 4:6-7
2nd Timothy 1:7
Earnest Pugh song "Rain on us" written by Daniel Edward II Moore, Daniel Moore
Bible.Org "The Mind Of God"
Colossians 3:2
Romans 8: 5-8
Matthew 28:19
Romans 12:2
Carolyn Cole interview with Bustle.com "Self-love is learning to love oneself"
Eric Rosenberg 5 things that can hold a person back from being a Mogul published by BET 2016

Book Cover design by Screenshot Studios Michelle Ignacia
Email: officialscreenshots@gmail.com

Photograph done by Rodney Pitts Photography:
Email muddog20@gmail.com

CPSIA information can be obtained
at www.ICGtesting.com
Printed in the USA
FSHW021833061020
74472FS